Children's rights
LEARNING BOOK

Deborah Harcourt

Pademelon Press

First published 2012 by Pademelon Press
PO Box 42, Mt Victoria NSW 2786
www.pademelonpress.com.au

Author: Harcourt, Deborah.
Title: Children's rights learning book / Deborah Harcourt.
ISBN: 9781876138394 (pbk.)

Subjects: 1. Children's rights—Australia.
            2. Children—Legal status, laws, etc.—Australia.

Dewey Number: 323.3520994

Printed by Ligare Book Printers

The paper this publication is printed on is in accordance with the rules of the Forest Stewardship Council®.
The FSC® promotes environmentally responsible, socially beneficial and economically viable management of the world's forests.

This is the teacher and the children having their photo taken to be on the front cover of the children's rights book.

The authors

Abby mia Amity

Elizabeth Murphy

Beth Ben

Kei

Josh Imogen

Declan

Deborah

Pippi Ollie

Hudson Alex zpppph

The OK Paper

One of the key processes when engaging children in research is to ensure that they are fully informed about the research project and that they give their consent to participation as willing and empowered co-researchers. In the children's rights project, the children were offered an initial introduction to myself (Deborah) as a researcher, my role at a university and why the project was of importance to me. The children were encouraged to ask questions, offer ideas on how they might be involved and the ways in which they could put forward views and opinions to the group. As the children became familiar with the project, they were invited to construct a written document that signified their willingness to participate as a co-researcher. This became known by the children as the 'OK paper'.

Elizabeth
The OK paper tells you that it is ok for us to work together. If we don't do the ok then it is not ok for you to talk to us.

The children were invited to give their consent to working with me each and every time the children and I worked together as researchers. In this way, affirmation of the children's willingness to participate was not seen as a one-off exercise, but viewed as an ongoing democratic dialogue. The children decided that it is important for you, as the reader, to see that they are ok with sharing their ideas with you.

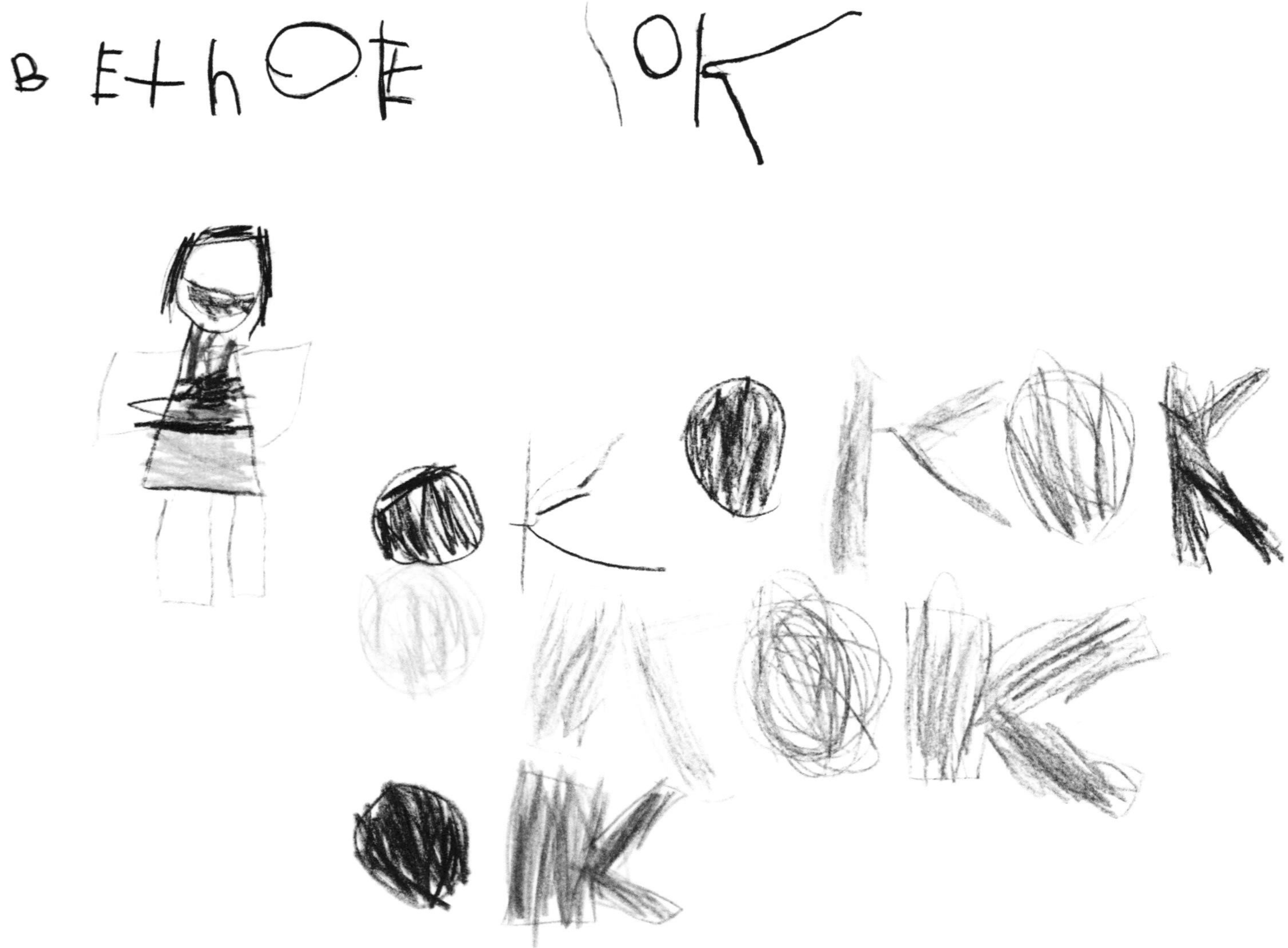

BEthOE 1OK
OK OKOK
AOK OK
OK

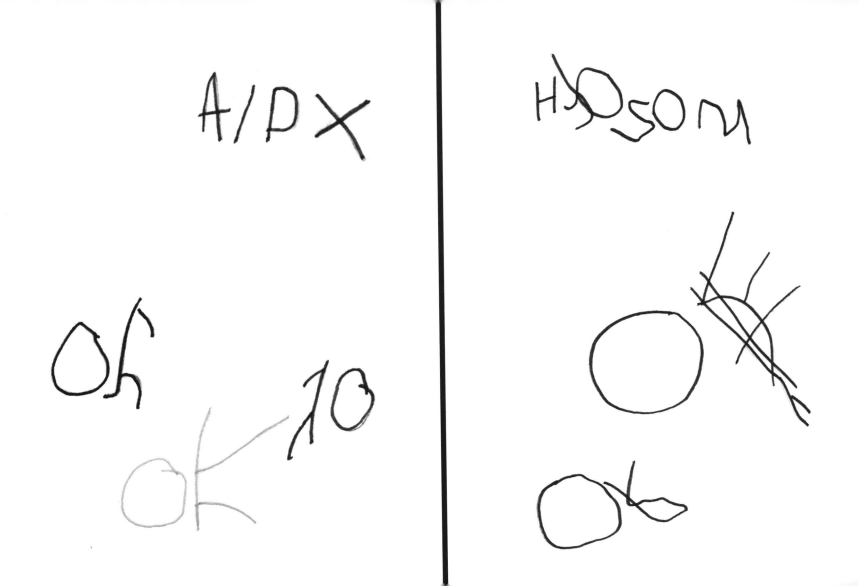

Decion

8 K OK
K
OK

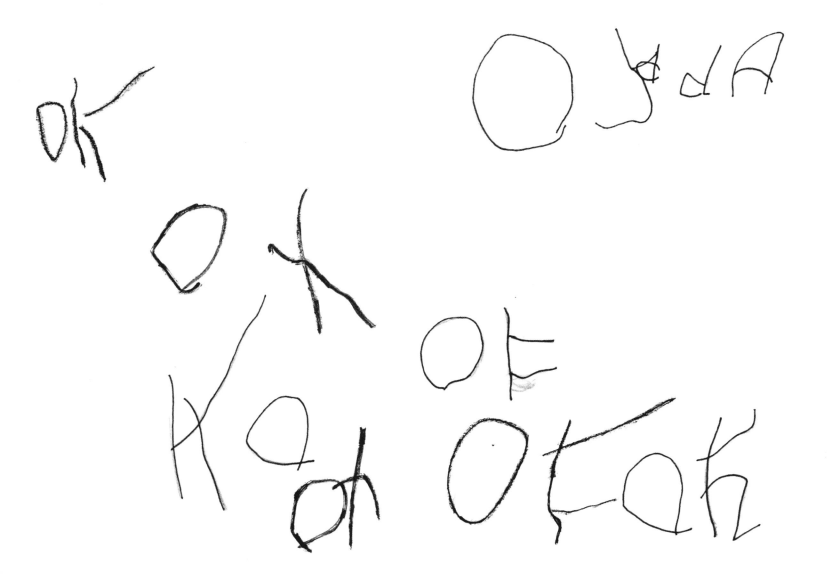

murphy

Pippi

KO

OK OK OK

EIIZADETHOK

TOSN

KO KO

OK

KO

kal

ka

mia ok   ko

OK OK

Sarah

Imogen

OK

OK

48

Ben

OE Ok

Ok Ok

Ollie

Children's rights is like being a superhero.

Abby

This book is about children's special ideas. They help you learn about children's rights.

Introducing the project

This project is one of the outcomes of the 2011 Jean Denton Memorial Scholarship. This was awarded to me (Deborah) to investigate whether the mandated rights under the United Nations Convention on the Rights of the Child are put into action by educators in children's everyday lives. As the project progressed, it became more apparent that the children, who were four and five years old, were constructing a set of rights that were more closely connected to their lived experience of childhood than the rhetorical rights as outlined in the Convention.

In discussions that occurred over a school year, the Investigators (as the children were known collectively) and I constructed an understanding on children's rights as viewed from the children's standpoint.

In the beginning, the children used complex drawings to guide their narratives about rights which were supported in small discussions. As the children developed over the year, many turning the milestone of five years old, the narratives became the stronger medium of sharing and the drawings became less of an anchor for their conversations.

The way in which this book has been constructed is as decided by the children. It is hoped that this book will sit apart from other books and pamphlets on children's rights as it is written by young children for young children and their teachers.

I would like to share a pivotal dialogue that occurred toward the end of the project, which will then lead you into the children's ideas about children's rights for your own consideration as an adult and, more importantly, so that other children may learn about children's rights too.

Imogen: *Are children's rights very important?*

Deborah: *What do you think?*

Imogen: *Yes, so they don't hurt themselves.*

Hudson: *... or get lost from their mum and dad.*

Declan: *And so they be safe.*

Imogen: *And so that they are not in danger from their mum and dad.*

Deborah: *I wonder if we should make a book together with all the ideas you have talked about?*

Mia: *Why?*

Elizabeth: *So that children who do not know about children's rights then we should give the book to them and then they will know.*

Mia: *Yes, so they know what we are saying and they can hear what we are saying.*

Sarah: *They might forget what their rights are.*

Elizabeth: *So if they come from far away, they could come to FELC and read our book and then they would know about children's rights. The children could talk to us because the teachers at FELC know about children's rights and they tell us about them.*

Children's rights as told by the children

Mia

Children have the right to share their toys with other people. They can share with their sisters and their mum. This is important because it is.

Abby

Children have the right to choose which swimming pool
they can go in because they might not like the decorations.
The decorations can be inviting. They make you feel happy.
Sometimes swimming classes aren't very exciting, so children
should be able to choose the right pool themselves.

Elizabeth

Children have the right to ask other children who have lots of
things if the other children who have lots of things to share.
If they didn't share then they are not being fair. If you share
this means they like you and want to be your friend.

Elizabeth

Amity

If you hurt yourself adults have to come and get you quickly.

Amity

Declan

Children have the right to be safe so they don't get lost so they don't get stolded.

Declan

Pippi

Children have the right to play. They can play with blocks, dollies, dress-ups and prams.

pippi

Imogen

Children have the right to be safe. If a big storm comes at the beach then the children know how to be safe themselves if their mum or dad is not there. Children can practise to be safe when they are at home, that's how they learn.

Murphy

Some children have their legs locked up. Adults need to take the locks off and they should take the children to their home.

Murpky

Joshua

I have tree rights. I have the right to climb up a tree using my hands.

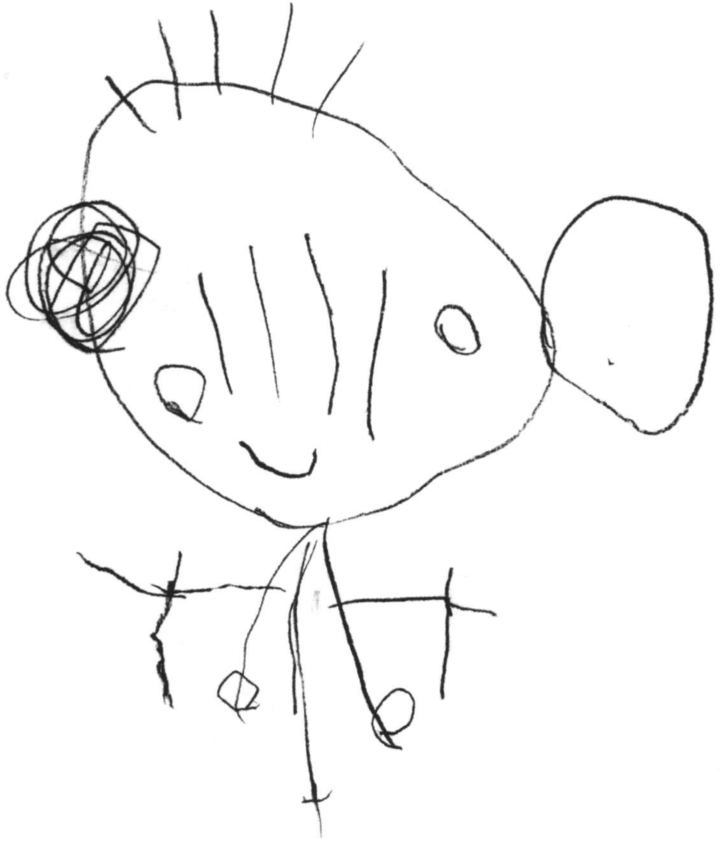

Kai

Children have the right to live. We waste too much food and all the people in the other countries don't have food. We need to send food on the food plane to help.

Kai

Beth

Children have the right to dream about going on a train because their mum never ever says they can go. The mum always says 'don't go'. Children don't know what a train looks like.

Sarah

Children have a right to be princesses and if they don't have a house they have children's rights to live in a castle.

Hudson

Children have the right to cross the road and hold mum or dad or your brother's hand. You need to stop and look both ways and look for cars coming. When there are no cars and the light turns red on the special pole then you can cross the road. You would get runned over if you crossed by yourself.

Hudson

Ben

Children have the right to live in a house with windows. They need to feel safe and not scared and they have the right to eat safe vegetables.

Ben

Alex

Children have the right to help a friend when you can do something that they can't do. If the other person can't do bowling I could help them because I can do bowling.

Alex

Ollie

This is a message. Just a small one. It says to the poor children, 'Wait, we are coming to help you.' They can send a message back. It might say, 'Please hurry.' We then need to go on an airplane and help them. We need to get rid of missolds too. That would be good.

This is the message I wrote. 'We are coming straight away.'

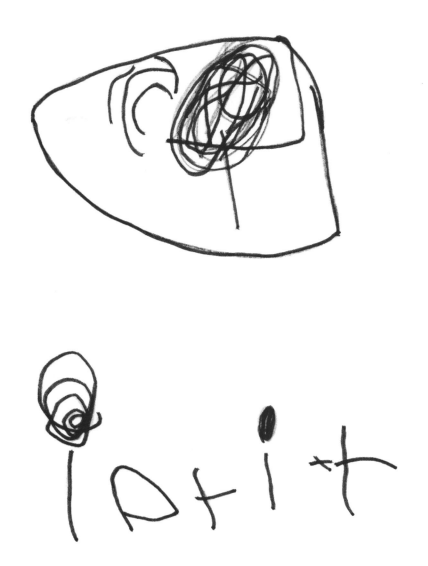

This is how you use our book

Joshua: *Look at it and read what it says.*

Kai: *It tells you when you go to a swimming pool you need a mum and dad to keep you safe.*

Elizabeth: *Please use the book carefully and gently coz you don't want to break it.*

Abby: *Teachers could learn from the book and discover what children can do.*

Elizabeth: *Speak carefully so the children can hear you.*

Abby: *We need to get grown-ups to like the book. They need to learn from the book.*

Sarah: *Read it and look at the pictures. Make sure you give it back to the teacher.*

Amity: *You could borrow the book from the library and take it home and read it to your mums and dads and brothers and babies and learn about children's rights.*

Hudson: *Don't snatch this book from someone who is reading it.*

Alex: *If you break this book then you won't learn anything.*

Declan: *You can look at the pictures if you can't read yet.*

Ollie: *Make sure you learn about children's rights.*

With thanks

I would particularly like to thank the children in the Investigators group from the Flinders Early Learning Centre (FELC) on the Sunshine Coast in Queensland for their extraordinary generosity in sharing their thoughts and ideas. Without them, we would not have an understanding of rights as a lived experience.

I would also like to pay tribute to the children's teachers, Cathy and Gail, for accepting the disruption of a researcher. A very special thank you to Vivienne, the Director, for her support, guidance and collegiality over the year of the project.

Additional thanks to the Jean Denton Memorial Scholarship committee for seeing the importance of this project and for providing funding for it to proceed.

To Professor Solveig Hägglund from Karlstad University in Sweden for her wise counsel and with whom I will be working on a similar study with 4-year-old children in her country in 2012.

I hope that teachers, parents and children are motivated to discuss children's rights together and remember that if you have any questions, the Investigators are very willing to help you learn.

Deborah Harcourt, Professor of Early Childhood, Australian Catholic University
October 2012

Remember

Children are watching us watching them!